STANDING ON HER SHOULDERS

A Celebration of Women

To those who came before me:
Phyllis,
Kathleen,
Verna Pearl,
Ruth,
Dolly,
and Lena

And to those who came after me:
Madeleine
and Beatrice

— M.C.R.

For my Angels, Jacqui and Roberta

— L.F.

Text copyright © 2021 by Monica Clark-Robinson
Illustrations copyright © 2021 by Laura Freeman

Library of Congress Cataloging-in-Publication Data Available

ISBN 978-1-338-35800-1

10 9 8 7 6 5 4 3 2 1   21 22 23 24 25

Printed in China   38
First edition, February 2021

Laura Freeman's illustrations were rendered digitally. The book was typeset in Adobe Caslon Pro, which was designed by Carol Twombly in 1990 — a revival of letterforms originally drawn by William Caslon. Book design by Brian LaRossa.

STANDING ON HER SHOULDERS

A Celebration of Women

BY MONICA CLARK-ROBINSON
ART BY LAURA FREEMAN

ORCHARD BOOKS • NEW YORK
an imprint of Scholastic Inc.

Come sit with us, child,
we have stories to tell.
Listen closely.
You come from a deep, deep well.

Our mothers and all those
who've gone before,
paved a freer path
and opened a wider door.

There's surely still plenty of work to do,
but there's much to learn
from what they went through.

For we are standing on the shoulders
of the strong, smart, sage, and soulful
ones who have gone before us.

Think of the one who mothers you.
She's with you, even when you are apart.
You are forever a piece of her heart.

Speak her name.

And the ones who came before her,
generations strong.
Their words sing of grit and love —
your family song.

Freedom seekers, truth speakers,
fierce women, brave and wise,
justice burning in their eyes.

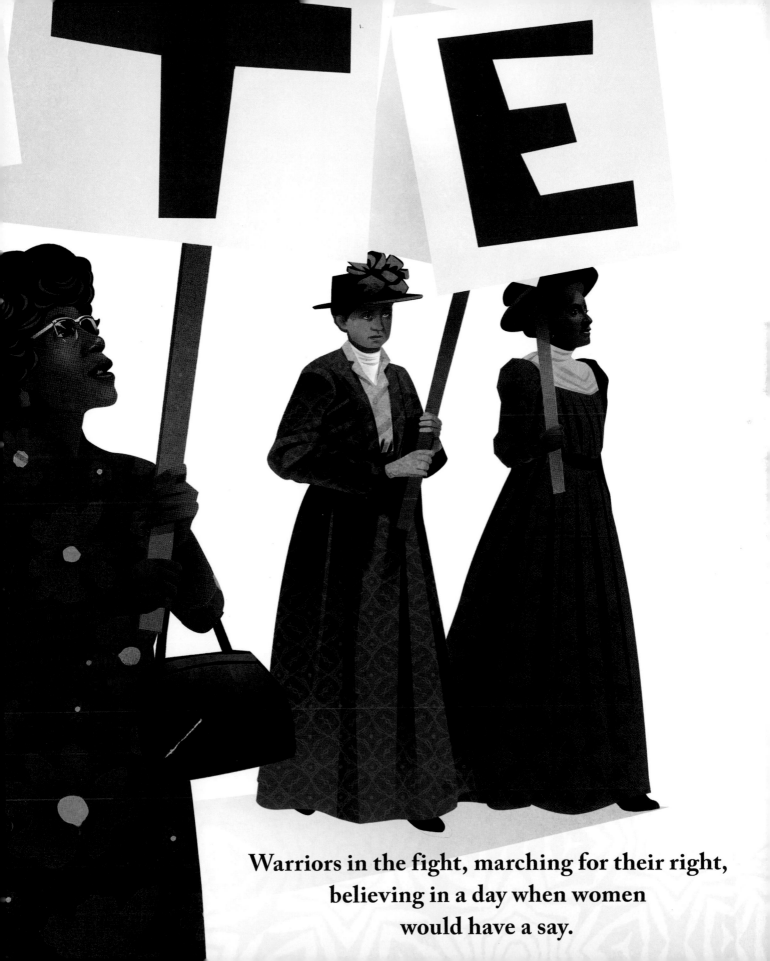

Warriors in the fight, marching for their right,
believing in a day when women
would have a say.

**Champions of equality,
challengers of authority,
peaceful freedom fighters,
brave and bold bus riders.**

Magic-believers,
dream weavers.
Revolutionary minds,
their works echoing
through time.

Keen and curious explorers,
refusing to take orders.
Women who dared to defy,
showing girls another way to fly.

We are
standing
on their
shoulders.

When we remember them and speak their names,
we respect the struggles they overcame.

We are grateful for the freedoms they've given.
We stand on the shoulders of powerful women.

Women who were little once . . .

Just like you.

When we speak, whisper, sing, and shout their names,
we honor their lives and the rights we gained.
We are ALL standing on their shoulders.

Who will stand on YOURS?

SERENA WILLIAMS 1981–
is a professional tennis player
who has won dozens of
Grand Slam titles and four
Olympic gold medals.

MEGAN RAPINOE 1985–
is a professional soccer player
and the co-captain of the gold
medal–winning United States
Women's National Team.

SIMONE BILES 1997–
holds the record for the most combined
World and Olympic medals in
gymnastics. She is currently America's
most decorated gymnast.

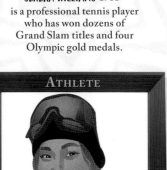

CHLOE KIM 2000–
became the youngest woman to win
an Olympic gold medal in snowboarding,
at age seventeen. She currently holds
the World Championship title in the
half-pipe category.

MARY CASSATT 1844–1926
was an Impressionist painter famous for
painting intimate portraits of the bond
between mother and child.

FRIDA KAHLO 1907–1954
was a Mexican painter known for
unflinching self-portraits, including
works painted after accidents that
caused her great pain.

GEORGIA O'KEEFFE 1887–1986
was a celebrated Modernist artist who
painted the world around her, from desert
flowers to city skylines.

FAITH RINGGOLD 1930–
is an artist, civil rights activist, and
author, best known for presenting stories
through quilted works of art.

HILLARY CLINTON 1947–
has held several US public roles,
including First Lady, US senator, and
secretary of state. In 2016, she became
the first woman to win the popular vote
in a presidential election.

POLITICIAN

DEB HAALAND 1960–

is an enrolled member of the Pueblo of Laguna and one of the first two Native American women elected to the US Congress.

POLITICIAN

SHIRLEY CHISHOLM 1924–2005

was the daughter of West Indian immigrants and the first African American woman elected to the US Congress. In 1972, she was the first Black candidate to run for a major party's nomination in the presidential election.

ACTIVIST

FANNIE LOU HAMER 1917–1977

was a civil rights and voting rights activist and an outspoken founding member of several civil rights organizations.

ACTIVIST

ROSA PARKS 1913–2005

was a civil rights activist famous for her strategic refusal to give up a bus seat in the "whites only" area of a city bus, spurring the Montgomery Bus Boycott.

ACTIVIST

MARY CHURCH TERRELL 1863–1954

was one of the first Black women to earn a college degree. She was a suffragist and a founding member of the NAACP.

ACTIVIST

JANE ADDAMS 1860–1935

was an activist and social worker who co-founded the American Civil Liberties Union. She was the first American woman to win the Nobel Peace Prize.

ACTIVIST

HARRIET TUBMAN 1822–1913

was a former enslaved woman who led 70 enslaved people to freedom as a conductor on the Underground Railroad. She also led raids that freed more than 700 enslaved people during the Civil War.

ACTIVIST

SOJOURNER TRUTH 1797–1883

was an orator, abolitionist, and suffragist who gave a famous speech titled "Ain't I a Woman" at a women's rights conference in Ohio.

EDUCATOR

SEPTIMA POINSETTE CLARK 1898–1987

was an activist and educator who created "citizenship schools," helping hundreds of thousands of Black citizens in the South learn to read and become legal voters.

AUTHOR

LOUISA MAY ALCOTT 1832–1888
was an abolitionist, feminist, and author. She wrote twenty novels, including the beloved Little Women series.

AUTHOR

MAYA ANGELOU 1928–2014
was a poet, author, and performer, most famous for her autobiography *I Know Why the Caged Bird Sings.*

AUTHOR

ZORA NEALE HURSTON 1891–1960
was an anthropologist and author who wrote about the African American experience. Her most famous novel was *Their Eyes Were Watching God.*

EXPLORER

SACAJAWEA 1788–1884
was a Lemhi Shoshone woman who was captured as a young girl and forced to marry a French-Canadian man. Later, she famously accompanied Lewis and Clark on their westward expedition as an interpreter and guide, carrying her young son the entire time.

EXPLORER

BESSIE COLEMAN 1892–1926
was an airplane pilot who was both the first African American and Native American woman to hold a pilot's license.

EXPLORER

NELLIE BLY 1864–1922
was a journalist who pioneered an investigative type of reporting, most famously taking a record-breaking solo trip around the world in 1889.

SCIENTIST

YNÉS MEXIA 1870–1938
was a Mexican American explorer and botanist who traveled the world cataloguing plants, including 500 new species.

SCIENTIST

HARRIET CHALMERS ADAMS 1875–1937
was an explorer and journalist who traveled the world extensively and wrote about her explorations for *National Geographic.*

AUTHOR'S NOTE

When I was preparing for the birth of my second daughter, a wise woman friend of mine told me to imagine the expanding circles of women behind me, supporting me. I imagined my friends, my elders, and my ancestors. I imagined the famous women throughout history who broke through walls and changed the world. I imagined, too, the daughter who would soon be born. This image of that unbroken chain is what first inspired *Standing On Her Shoulders*.

Though we still have far to go in our efforts at true equality, how very far we have come! The freedoms we enjoy today were hard-won by those in the past. They may not have been perfect, but they were the fierce warriors we needed. Remembering their lives and speaking their names is the least we can do to honor their legacy.

One of my goals as a woman, mother, and writer is to be a strong set of shoulders for the future to stand on. Together, we are stronger and smarter and braver and kinder than any one of us is alone. We are what the world needs.

You are exactly what our future needs.

ILLUSTRATOR'S NOTE

It was an honor to be asked to illustrate *Standing On Her Shoulders*. It was a long time in the making, but I loved this beautifully written manuscript as soon as I read it. One of the best things about this wonderful job that I do is that I am constantly learning new things. As the editors suggested women to include in my illustrations, I found myself researching and learning more about some of the inspirational women I already knew of and meeting some really amazing women from history I had never even heard of! I hope this book inspires kids to do their own research and learn more about these women, especially those not so widely known, women like Mary Church Terrell and Ynés Mexia. I thought I was familiar with Maya Angelou's work, but before starting on this book, I had no idea that she used to be a dancer. I love finding out things like that!

My pictures tell the story from the perspective of three generations of a small family who pass women's history (along with the history of their own family) down to their daughters. I hope it inspires you to do the same.

AUTHOR'S ACKNOWLEDGMENTS

As always, I rely on the brilliant women of my critique group, especially my dear Heather and Amelia.

I'm grateful for the support of my family — My parents, Greg, Maddie, Bee, and Josh, among others. Thanks for believing in me.

Thanks also to my wonderful agent, Natalie Lakosil, and both of the terrific Scholastic editors who worked on this book, Orli Zuravicky and Katie Heit.

ILLUSTRATOR'S ACKNOWLEDGMENTS

Thank you to all the women on whose shoulders I've stood. It's because of you that I've realized my dreams.